LIVING WITH DISEASES AND DISORDERS

Cerebral Palsy and Other Traumatic Brain Injuries

LIVING WITH DISEASES AND DISORDERS

ADHD and Other Behavior Disorders

Allergies and Other Immune System Disorders

Asthma, Cystic Fibrosis, and Other Respiratory Disorders

Autism and Other Developmental Disorders

Cancer and Sickle Cell Disease

Cerebral Palsy and Other Traumatic Brain Injuries

Crohn's Disease and Other Digestive Disorders

Depression, Anxiety, and Bipolar Disorders

Diabetes and Other Endocrine Disorders

Migraines and Seizures

Muscular Dystrophy and Other Neuromuscular Disorders

LIVING WITH DISEASES AND DISORDERS

Cerebral Palsy and Other Traumatic Brain Injuries

REBECCA SHERMAN

SERIES ADVISOR

HEATHER L. PELLETIER, Ph.D.

Pediatric Psychologist, Hasbro Children's Hospital

Clinical Assistant Professor, Warren Alpert Medical School of Brown University

MASON CREST

Mason Crest
450 Parkway Drive, Suite D
Broomall, PA 19008
www.masoncrest.com

MTM Publishing, Inc.
435 West 23rd Street, #8C
New York, NY 10011
www.mtmpublishing.com

President: Valerie Tomaselli
Vice President, Book Development: Hilary Poole
Designer: Annemarie Redmond
Copyeditor: Peter Jaskowiak
Editorial Assistant: Leigh Eron

Series ISBN: 978-1-4222-3747-2
Hardback ISBN: 978-1-4222-3753-3
E-Book ISBN: 978-1-4222-8034-8

Library of Congress Cataloging-in-Publication Data
Names: Sherman, Rebecca, author.
Title: Cerebral palsy and other traumatic brain disorders / by Rebecca Sherman; series consultant, Heather Pelletier, PhD Hasbro Children's Hospital, Alpert Medical School/ Brown University.
Description: Broomall, PA: Mason Crest, [2018] | Series: Living with diseases and disorders | Audience: 12+ | Audience: Grade 7 to 8. | Includes index.
Identifiers: LCCN 2017007140 (print) | LCCN 2017007930 (ebook) | ISBN9781422237533 (hardback : alk. paper) | ISBN 9781422280348 (ebook)
Subjects: LCSH: Cerebral palsy—Juvenile literature.
Classification: LCC RC388 .S438 2018 (print) | LCC RC388 (ebook) | DDC 616.8/36—dc23
LC record available at https://lccn.loc.gov/2017007140

Printed and bound in the United States of America.

First printing
9 8 7 6 5 4 3 2 1

QR CODES AND LINKS TO THIRD PARTY CONTENT
You may gain access to certain third party content ("Third Party Sites") by scanning and using the QR Codes that appear in this publication (the "QR Codes"). We do not operate or control in any respect any information, products or services on such Third Party Sites linked to by us via the QR Codes included in this publication and we assume no responsibility for any materials you may access using the QR Codes. Your use of the QR Codes may be subject to terms, limitations, or restrictions set forth in the applicable terms of use or otherwise established by the owners of the Third Party Sites. Our linking to such Third Party Sites via the QR Codes does not imply an endorsement or sponsorship of such Third Party Sites, or the information, products or services offered on or through the Third Party Sites, nor does it imply an endorsement or sponsorship of this publication by the owners of such Third Party Sites.

TABLE OF CONTENTS

Series Introduction 6

Chapter One: Meet Your Brain 9

Chapter Two: Cerebral Palsy 23

Chapter Three: Traumatic Brain Injury 37

Chapter Four: Living with CP or TBI. 49

Further Reading 57

Series Glossary 58

Index 60

About the Advisor. 64

About the Author 64

Photo Credits 64

Key Icons to Look for:

 Words to Understand: These words with their easy-to-understand definitions will increase the reader's understanding of the text, while building vocabulary skills.

 Sidebars: This boxed material within the main text allows readers to build knowledge, gain insights, explore possibilities, and broaden their perspectives by weaving together additional information to provide realistic and holistic perspectives.

 Educational Videos: Readers can view videos by scanning our QR codes, which will provide them with additional educational content to supplement the text. Examples include news coverage, moments in history, speeches, iconic sports moments, and much more.

 Text-Dependent Questions: These questions send the reader back to the text for more careful attention to the evidence presented there.

 Research Projects: Readers are pointed toward areas of further inquiry connected to each chapter. Suggestions are provided for projects that encourage deeper research and analysis.

 Series Glossary of Key Terms: This back-of-the-book glossary contains terminology used throughout the series. Words found here increase the reader's ability to read and comprehend higher-level books and articles in this field.

SERIES INTRODUCTION

According to the Chronic Disease Center at the Centers for Disease Control and Prevention, over 100 million Americans suffer from a chronic illness or medical condition. In other words, they have a health problem that lasts three months or more, affects their ability to perform normal activities, and requires frequent medical care and/or hospitalizations. Epidemiological studies suggest that between 15 and 18 million of those with chronic illness or medical conditions are children and adolescents. That's roughly one out of every four children in the United States.

These young people must exert more time and energy to complete the tasks their peers do with minimal thought. For example, kids with Crohn's disease, ulcerative colitis, or other digestive issues have to plan meals and snacks carefully, to make sure they are not eating food that could irritate their stomachs or cause pain and discomfort. People with cerebral palsy, muscular dystrophy, or other physical limitations associated with a medical condition may need help getting dressed, using the bathroom, or joining an activity in gym class. Those with cystic fibrosis, asthma, or epilepsy may have to avoid certain activities or environments altogether. ADHD and other behavior disorders require the individual to work harder to sustain the level of attention and focus necessary to keep up in school.

Living with a chronic illness or medical condition is not easy. Identifying a diagnosis and adjusting to the initial shock is only the beginning of a long journey. Medications, follow-up appointments and procedures, missed school or work, adjusting to treatment regimens, coping with uncertainty, and readjusting expectations are all hurdles one has to overcome in learning how to live one's best life. Naturally, feelings of sadness or anxiety may set in while learning how to make it all work. This is especially true for young people, who may reach a point in their medical journey when they have to rethink some of their original goals and life plans to better match their health reality.

Chances are, you know people who live this reality on a regular basis. It is important to remember that those affected by chronic illness are family members, neighbors, friends, or maybe even our own doctors. They are likely navigating the demands of the day a little differently, as they balance the specific accommodations necessary to manage their illness. But they have the same desire to be productive and included as those who are fortunate not to have a chronic illness.

This set provides valuable information about the most common childhood chronic illnesses, in language that is engaging and easy for students to grasp. Each chapter highlights important vocabulary words and offers text-dependent questions to help assess comprehension. Meanwhile, educational videos (available by scanning QR codes) and research projects help connect the text to the outside world.

Our mission with this set is twofold. First, the volumes provide a go-to source for information about chronic illness for young people who are living with particular conditions. Each volume in this set strives to provide reliable medical information and practical advice for living day-to-day with various challenges. Second, we hope these volumes will also help kids without chronic illness better understand and appreciate how people with health challenges live. After all, if one in four young people is managing a health condition, it's safe to assume that the majority of our youth already know someone with a chronic illness, whether they realize it or not.

With the growing presence of social media, bullying is easier than ever before. It's vital that young people take a moment to stop and think about how they are more similar to kids with health challenges than they are different. Poor understanding and low tolerance for individual differences are often the platforms for bullying and noninclusive behavior, both in person and online. Living with Diseases and Disorders strives to close the gap of misunderstanding.

The ultimate solution to the bullying problem is surely an increase in empathy. We hope these books will help readers better understand and appreciate not only the daily struggles of people living with chronic conditions, but their triumphs as well.

—Heather Pelletier, Ph.D.
Hasbro Children's Hospital
Warren Alpert Medical School of Brown University

WORDS TO UNDERSTAND

axon: part of a neuron that extends out and carries signals to other cells.

capillaries: tiny blood vessels that carry blood from larger blood vessels to body tissues.

congenital: a condition or disorder that exists from birth.

contusions: bruises.

dendrites: part of a neuron that extends out and receives signals from other cells.

diffuse: widespread, all over the place.

focal: limited to a well-defined site, localized.

glia, or glial cells: several types of cells that support and protect neurons.

hematoma: a mass formed by blood clots.

hemorrhage: bleeding from a broken blood vessel.

meninges: protective membranes around the brain and spinal cord.

motor disabilities: impaired ability to move and control muscles.

nerves: bundles of axons.

neurons: specialized cells found in the central nervous system (the brain and spinal cord).

CHAPTER ONE

Meet Your Brain

Think about what you're going to have for lunch. Or about what your teacher just wrote on the board. Or something your friend told you between classes.

Your brain is where all these thoughts take place. But your brain does so much more than think your conscious thoughts. The command center of your body, it controls almost everything you do. Without you even being aware of it, your brain silently commands your interactions with the world around you. All the information you collect with your senses is useless to you until your brain makes sense of it. Your eyes don't work without your brain. Neither do your ears, or even your mouth. When you're using language, gestures, pictures, or music to communicate, your brain is in charge.

Your brain controls all of your voluntary muscle movements: walking, running, picking up a pencil, bringing a forkful of macaroni to your mouth, even chewing and swallowing your food. What's more, your brain manages to juggle all these vital tasks simultaneously. If you can walk, talk, and chew gum at the same time, you can thank your brain.

Whether you are aware of it or not, every physical action you take requires instructions from the brain.

Inside Your Head

The brain manages all these tasks by sending commands and messages using special cells called **neurons**. Like tiny communication devices, neurons "talk" to one another using electrical signals and chemicals called neurotransmitters. The cell body of the neuron sends these signals down a long, thin extension called an **axon**. Axons, which when bundled together are called **nerves**, are like the electrical cables of your brain and central nervous system. Some axons are up to three feet long!

At the other end of the axon, the messages are received by a different kind of extension that branches out from other neurons. These branching receptors are called **dendrites**, and they look kind of like trees. Neurons are the only kind of cells that have axons and dendrites. And neurons are unique in another way. While other kinds of cells in your body wear out, die, and are replaced all the time,

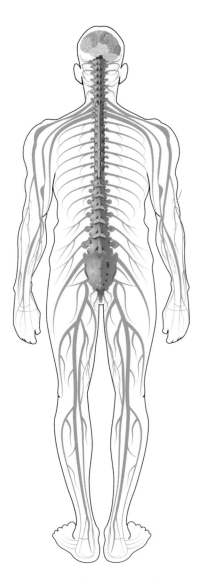

Your brain communicates with the rest of your body via the nervous system. Messages travel from your brain down your spinal cord in the middle of your back. From there messages travel all over a network called the peripheral nervous system.

THE STRUCTURES OF THE BRAIN

Your cerebrum is the largest and most complex part of your brain. It's divided into two hemispheres, right and left, with similar structures on each side. Each hemisphere is further divided into four lobes, each with many overlapping functions.

The cerebral cortex is the outer part of the cerebrum. It contains a lot of the main bodies of neurons, and is sometimes known as "gray matter." This name distinguishes it from white matter, the parts of the brain that get their color from the white fatty insulation that protects axons extending from the neurons.

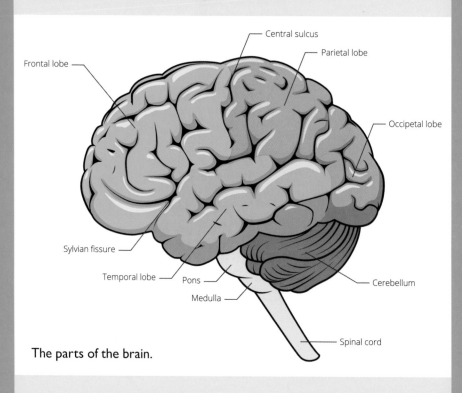

The parts of the brain.

your neurons have to last your whole lifetime. To help them last over the long haul, they are supported and protected by a different type of cells, called **glial cells**.

Some neurons send messages to other neurons in the brain. Others send messages down your spinal cord, to be delivered to your muscles. Still others communicate with your eyes, your ears, and your other senses. Different regions of the brain have different responsibilities. For example, two areas at the back of the brain, called the occipital lobes, are in charge of making sense of what you see. If your occipital lobes got damaged, you might lose your sight.

The brain is protected with several layers of tough and cushioning material. The thick bone covering that makes up the top and back of your head is your skull. Underneath the skull, the brain is further protected by three layers of waterproof membrane known as the **meninges**. The thick outermost layer is called the *dura mater*—a Latin phrase that translates to "tough mother"! The middle layer looks something like a spider web and is called the *arachnoid mater*. The innermost layer, the *pia mater* (or "tender mother," in Latin), covers and protects the surface of the brain itself. Together, the skull and the membranes shield the brain from things that might damage it. One of the things that the brain must be protected from is your own blood! Blood is toxic to brain cells. The meninges forms a barrier between the blood and the brain, allowing fluid and nutrients to reach brain cells, but keeping out the toxic components of blood.

Injuries to the Brain

Unlike the rest of your body, the brain has limited ability to replace vital cells if they cells die or are badly damaged. That's why an injury to the brain may cause a person to permanently lose the ability to do certain things. Some brain injuries affect a person's ability to think or remember previous experiences. Other brain injuries impair movement and coordination. Brain injuries can prevent someone from walking or talking. They can deprive a person of the use of one or both arms and legs. Brain injuries can make you see double, or have blurry vision. They can create a constant ringing sound in a person's ears. An injury to the brain can change how a person feels and behaves. It can make someone depressed, anxious, irritable, impulsive, or aggressive.

Brain injuries have many different causes. A brain injury may occur before a person is even born, very late in a person's life, or at any time in between. Some injuries may have effects that are temporary, or they may cause very little impairment in a person's ability to function. On the other end of the scale, very severe brain injuries can completely disable or even kill a person.

Brain injuries of all kinds are surprisingly common, especially in kids. Some kinds of brain damage are caused by something that goes wrong while a

Brain injuries can happen at any age; young athletes can be especially vulnerable.

fetus is developing in the womb. Brain damage can also occur while a baby is being born. These kinds of brain injuries are called **congenital** brain damage. Cerebral palsy (CP), a disorder that affects a person's ability to control his or her movements, is usually the result of congenital brain damage to an area of the brain called the cerebral cortex. This part of the brain plays a big role in the ability to tell your muscles how to move.

EDUCATIONAL VIDEO

Scan this code to watch a video about the brain and how injuries affect it.

Cerebral palsy is the main cause of **motor disabilities** in kids.

Traumatic brain injuries (TBIs) are another form of brain damage that affects kids, and people of all ages. TBIs kill more than 50,000 people every year in the United States. Many more people suffer some kind of temporary or permanent disability from less severe TBIs, like concussions. Some 2.2 million people visit emergency rooms every year suffering from the symptoms of a concussion. Most concussions are mild injuries, but repeated concussions can create very serious and permanent damage in the brain.

The Where, When, and How of Brain Injuries

What a brain injury does to a person depends on many factors. A brain injury is categorized by what causes the injury, where the injury is located, and how much damage the injury creates. Brain injuries are often described as mild, moderate, or severe.

Congenital brain damage may have many different causes, some of which remain poorly understood. In some cases, one or more mutations in the genes

15

that control brain development give the wrong instructions to the developing fetus, creating brain damage. These mutations may be inherited, or they may happen randomly. In other cases, delicate blood vessels in the fetus's developing brain may break, causing bleeding in the brain. If a pregnant woman is infected by certain viruses or bacteria, the infection may damage the fetal brain. If the fetus doesn't receive enough of certain nutrients, the brain may not develop normally. Finally, if the supply of oxygen to the fetus is cut off for any length of time, the brain may be damaged.

Traumatic brain injury (TBI) describes any damage that the brain suffers after birth due to external forces, like a blow to the head or shock waves from an explosion. These forces can crack the layers of protection surrounding your brain. Think about what happens if you accidentally drop an apple. Sometimes the force of the apple hitting the ground breaks open the apple's protective skin, and the flesh of the apple gets contaminated with dirt. The same thing can happen if the head receives a severe blow. The protective layers surrounding the brain are breached, allowing a foreign object to make contact with brain tissue. In this type of skull fracture, the bones of the skull break such that they actually touch the tissue of the brain, causing damage. More generally, these devastating types of contact injuries to the brain are called *penetrating TBIs*. They can result from gunshot wounds, crushing blows, or high-speed crashes.

In *non-penetrating TBIs*, the protection around the brain remains intact, but the shock waves from a blow or explosion cause the brain to move around within the skull. This damages the brain's delicate tissues. You can't necessarily see any sign of a non-penetrating TBI. Think again of a dropped apple. You might pick it up, wash it off, and bite into it. Then you discover that the flesh of the apple inside is brown and softened, damaged from the force of the fall. Something similar can happen to the brain.

Sports injuries often result in non-penetrating TBIs. Concussions are the most common type of non-penetrating TBI. A doctor or other trained person judges

Car accidents are a fairly common cause of brain injuries.

whether someone has a concussion following a blow to the head based on the symptoms the person experiences, rather than on any sign of visible injury.

Types of Brain Injuries

When an injury is localized, or confined to one or more well-defined areas of the brain, it's known as a **focal** injury. Penetrating TBIs often result in focal injuries. Non-penetrating TBIs tend to cause more widespread damage in the brain, and are

Medical researchers are concerned that young soccer players can injure their brains when heading the ball.

called **diffuse** injuries. But both categories of injury can be present at once. There are several different types of damage the brain can suffer, including the following:

- **Diffuse axonal injuries (DAIs).** DAIs occur when bundles of axons in the brain get twisted back and forth because of immense forces affecting the brain, like when someone traveling at high speed comes to a sudden stop during a crash. DAIs are also common in sports injuries, which can involve high speeds and twisting, rotational forces capable of damaging or even shearing axons. Just like a badly twisted power cord can short out and stop connecting, axons subjected to rotational forces can stop connecting to neurons and fail to send messages. They can also flood neurons with neurotransmitters, like a frayed cord emitting a shower of sparks. It can take a long time to recover from these injuries, and the damage can sometimes be permanent.

- **Hemorrhages and hematomas.** If blood vessels are damaged such that blood leaks into surrounding tissues, that is called a **hemorrhage**. A **hematoma** takes place if the leaking blood pools and forms a mass. Epidermal hematomas create bleeding in the area between the skull and the dura mater. Subdural hematomas cause blood to pool between the dura mater and the arachnoid mater. Subarachnoid hemorrhages bleed between the arachnoid mater and the pia mater. All of these can cause damage to the brain by pressing down or exerting pressure on brain tissue. An intracerebral hematoma bleeds directly into the brain itself.

- **Contusions.** This is a name for bleeding and swelling that occurs when very tiny blood vessels, called **capillaries**, leak blood. You may know **contusions** by their more common name: bruises. Coup lesions are bruises in the brain that occur directly underneath where a blow landed. Contrecoup lesions are bruises that form on the opposite side of the brain from where the blow hit.

The damage that occurs immediately as a result of a blow or shock waves is known as a primary injury. A secondary injury can occur hours, days, weeks, or even months later as a consequence of the primary injury. For example, if a

THE PALSIED KING?

Physicians used to believe that babies with brain damage either died at birth or completely recovered. A 19th-century British physician named William John Little was the first person to suggest that brain damage at or before birth could cause the motor disabilities we now call cerebral palsy. For evidence, he pointed not just to medical observations, but also to the words of Shakespeare. In the opening monologue of his play *Richard III*, Shakespeare described the 15th-century king this way:

> *Deform'd, unfinish'd, sent before my time*
> *Into this breathing world, scarce half made up,*
> *And that so lamely and unfashionable*
> *That dogs bark at me, as I halt by them.*

These words, along with descriptions of the king having a limp and a withered arm, seemed to provide evidence that Richard III had CP.

All that changed in 2012, thanks to the discovery of the long-lost skeleton of Richard III under a parking lot in the English city of Leicester. It showed that the king did indeed have severe scoliosis, a spinal deformity often associated with CP. But he did not have any signs of weakness or atrophy in his arms or legs. That means it's unlikely that he had CP.

Richard III can still serve as an example of the dangers of brain damage, though. His skeleton shows that, in his final battle, he suffered skull fractures that caused a TBI severe enough to kill him.

Pictured above: a portrait of King Richard III.

contusion continues to leak small blood over time, enough blood may eventually pool to form a hematoma.

Edema, or swelling in the brain, causes the brain to expand, creating high pressures that may cause a secondary injury by cutting off blood flow and oxygen to the brain. Secondary injuries are the reason why doctors want to monitor someone for continuing or new symptoms even after a mild primary injury, like a concussion.

Text-Dependent Questions

1. How are neurons unique?
2. List three ways that brain injuries can affect someone.
3. What kind of injury is a concussion?

Research Project

Phineas Gage had a hole blown through his head in 1845, long before modern medicine learned to treat TBI. Read more about his story here: https://www.verywell.com/phineas-gage-2795244.

WORDS TO UNDERSTAND

ataxia: a reduction in or loss of the ability to move muscles voluntarily.

athetoid: involuntary writhing movements caused by muscle contractions.

choreic: sudden jerky movements caused by muscle spasms.

chronic: long-lasting, usually lifelong.

contracture: when muscles or tendons get tight or hard, preventing movement.

hypoxia: not enough oxygen.

ischemic injury: injury caused by the blood supply being cut off.

orthopedic: dealing with deformities in bones or muscles.

orthotic devices: supports or braces for arms, legs, or the spine.

paresis: muscle weakness or partial paralysis.

-plegia: a suffix meaning "paralysis."

seizure: a sudden attack of symptoms or illness relating to abnormal signaling activity in the brain.

stroke: a sudden attack of symptoms or disability caused by abnormal blood flow to the brain.

CHAPTER TWO

Cerebral Palsy

More than 1 in every 300 babies born in the United States has some form of cerebral palsy (CP). If all the people in the world with cerebral palsy had their own country, it would have a population as large as the Netherlands—17 million people. It would be a diverse country, representing people with a wide range of abilities.

People with CP all share some degree of **ataxia**, an impairment in the ability to make voluntary movements. But this impairment can be very different from one person to another. Some people have trouble using their legs, their arms, or both. Some are impaired on one side of the body but not the other. Many people with CP have impairments of the muscles in their mouths, tongues, and throats. Some kids can reduce or even largely overcome their ataxia through treatment and therapy. Other kids, more severely affected, remain significantly impaired for their entire lives.

Risk Factors

Each kid with cerebral palsy has a unique set of abilities and challenges. But, taken as a whole, kids with CP have some things in common with one another.

Australian swimmer Priya Cooper celebrates her 1996 medal at the Paralympic Games in Atlanta. Cooper was born with CP, but she became a champion swimmer nonetheless.

Compared to people without CP, a larger percentage of kids with CP were born prematurely. They are more likely to have weighed less than five pounds at birth. They are more likely to have a twin, or be one of triplets. Being born prematurely, being very small at birth, and being one of a multiple birth are all risk factors for cerebral palsy. (*Risk factors* describe conditions that are more commonly found in people who have a certain disease than in people who don't have it.)

Risk factors matter most when you're looking at large numbers of people. Any individual kid might have none of the risk factors, but still have CP. Another kid might have all of those risk factors, but not have CP. Risk factors point the way toward conditions that doctors and scientists should research to learn more about what might cause a disease. But they are not themselves the causes.

Causes of Cerebral Palsy

We are still learning about the root causes of CP, the reasons why a baby's cerebral cortex gets damaged. In most individual cases, doctors don't know exactly why a baby gets CP. We do know that certain problems during labor and delivery can harm the brain while the baby is being born. Doctors used to believe that these problems were the cause of most cases of CP. Since then we have learned that they create a relatively small percentage of cases, around 20 percent. Another 70 percent of cases occur because of one or more conditions arising during pregnancy. For example, if the mother's blood type is different from that of the fetus, the mother's immune system may attack the fetus, causing brain damage.

Brain damage is also associated with certain infections and high fevers during pregnancy. Some of these infections cause few or no symptoms in adults. German measles, also known as rubella, is a mild disease in adults, but it produces numerous birth defects, including CP, in a fetus. Birth defects from German measles used to be widespread, but they are rare now thanks to laws requiring people to be vaccinated against the disease.

Other diseases linked to an increased risk of CP remain extraordinarily common. Toxoplasmosis, a parasitic disease that seems to increase the risk of CP, is present in nearly a quarter of Americans. Cytomegalovirus, another infection linked to CP, affects over half of all Americans at some point in life. Since these diseases are much more common than CP, scientists believe that they interact with other factors to determine whether or not a fetus develops CP. The timing of the infection may play a role; that is, a fetus is more vulnerable at certain stages of development.

New research suggests that some genetic mutations may also make a fetus more susceptible to brain damage from infection or to brain injuries from other causes, like **strokes**. A stroke is an interruption of the blood supply to the brain. Blood clots blocking blood vessels can lead to a stroke. So can weakened or broken blood vessels, or problems with the placenta that delivers blood, nutrients, and oxygen from the mother to the fetus. **Hypoxia**, or oxygen deprivation, causes brain damage at any age, but particularly in the vulnerable brain of a fetus or newborn.

Ischemic injury is the term for the damage done to tissues deprived of blood. Periventricular leukomalacia (PVL) is a common ischemic injury in premature infants. PVL damages a type of glial cell, the oligodendrocytes, in the brain of a developing fetus. Babies born with PVL are at much higher risk for being diagnosed with CP later on.

Diagnosis and Symptoms

Kids with CP have problems with muscle tone. These problems may be in one arm or leg, on one side of the body, or they can be widespread. Affected muscles may be too stiff and tight, resisting attempts to move them. The muscles might be overactive, flailing around involuntarily at the slightest trigger. Muscles can lock up into painful positions, a condition known as **contracture**. Any of these problems cause motor disabilities.

ACQUIRED CEREBRAL PALSY

Up to 10 percent of kids with CP have it as a result of brain damage that happened to them after they were born. Called acquired cerebral palsy, it can happen due to accidental head injuries sustained in a car accident or a bad fall. But in some tragic cases, the cause is abuse. Abuse can take the form of a blow to an infant's head, or it can be a case of shaken baby syndrome.

When babies are very young, the muscles in their necks haven't developed enough to support their heads. They can't hold their heads up without support. An adult holding a very young infant has to take care to gently support the baby's head. But some people aren't always careful. They might be exhausted, angry, or impaired by drugs or alcohol. Whatever the reason, if someone shakes an infant, the baby's head can snap back and forth so violently that the baby's brain is permanently damaged. This is why it's vitally important to keep your cool when taking care of a baby. A few seconds of anger can cause a disability that lasts the entire life.

Up to 90 percent of CP is congenital. But because even healthy newborns and infants don't have the ability to perform many voluntary movements, the symptoms of CP may not appear until a baby is old enough to be rolling over, sitting up, crawling, or walking. Most kids with CP are diagnosed by their second birthday. There's no blood test for CP. To make a diagnosis, doctors look for a combination of symptoms, delayed developmental milestones, and evidence of brain damage, as shown by brain scans or imaging.

A baby that doesn't learn to crawl or walk by the usual age might be evaluated for CP. So might a baby who can't bring her hands to her mouth, or who only uses one hand while his other hand remains clenched in a fist. Not gaining weight or being unusually short for one's age are also possible signs of CP. The symptoms of CP vary in type and severity from person to person. In any

BRAIN SCANS AND IMAGING

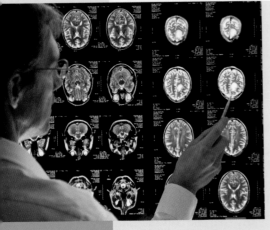

To confirm a diagnosis of CP, doctors rely on one or more of these ways to see inside a person's head:

- **Cranial ultrasound.** This technique uses high-frequency sound waves to create an image of the brain. But sound waves can't travel through bone, so it can only be used on newborns and young infants, whose skulls haven't fused yet.
- **Computed tomography.** Commonly known as a CT ("cat") scan, this procedure combines a series of X-rays, each taken of a focused, narrow area. Altogether, the data produced by the series of X-rays creates a three-dimensional image that's quite a bit clearer than a cranial ultrasound.
- **Magnetic resonance imaging (MRI).** This space-age technique produces very detailed three-dimensional images based on the responses of subatomic particles in the body's tissues to strong magnetic fields and radio waves. An MRI is often the best choice to diagnose brain injuries.

Some people with CP rely on assistive technology, such as wheelchairs, to get around.

given person, the symptoms are generally stable—they don't get any worse. If symptoms are getting progressively worse, they are probably the result of some condition other than CP.

Types of Cerebral Palsy

Three main types of CP are recognized, each with characteristic symptoms. These are described below.

Spastic CP affects from 70 to 80 percent of people with CP. The word *spastic* refers to spasms in which affected muscles become stiff or tight. These muscles are hard to move, and they are awkward in motion. They are described as being affected by **paresis**, meaning palsy or weakness, or **-plegia**, a suffix meaning paralysis. Kids with spastic hemiplegia or spastic hemiparesis have trouble controlling muscles on one side of the body. In some cases the problem is with one arm and hand. In other cases, the leg on the same side is also affected. The limbs on the affected side are often smaller or thinner than those on the other side. Kids may also develop scoliosis, an abnormal curving of the spine, as they grow.

Spastic diplegia and spastic diparesis create muscles stiffness in both legs. Kids with this variety of CP may need a walker or leg braces to aid them in getting around. Most kids with spastic hemiplegia/hemiparesis or spastic diplegia/diparesis have normal or above normal intelligence, but they may have some difficulty speaking clearly enough to be understood.

Spastic quadriplegia and spastic quadriparesis are the most disabling forms of CP—the prefix "quad-" means that all four limbs are affected. People with

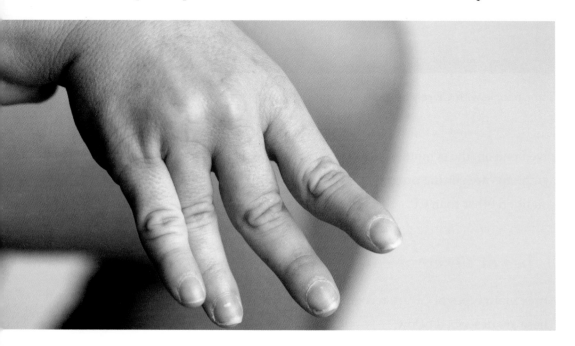

The spastic (meaning, "having spasms") hand of someone with CP.

quadriplegia or quadriparesis have severe brain damage, and may suffer from intellectual disabilities as well as physical impairments. Most are unable to walk, and many have trouble communicating. Epilepsy, a **seizure** disorder, is common in kids with spastic CP.

Dyskinetic CP, also known as athetoid CP, causes a person to make involuntary movements.

EDUCATIONAL VIDEO

Scan this code to watch a video about a teenage boy who has CP.

Athetoid movements are slow and writhing. **Choreic** movements are sudden and jerky. They get worse when a kid is excited, and subside while a kid is asleep. Muscles in the mouth and tongue may be affected, making it hard to speak. It can also cause uncontrollable drooling.

Ataxic CP makes it hard to balance. Kids with ataxic CP may have trouble with depth perception, the process by which the brain judges distances based on information from the eyes. People with ataxic CP may walk unsteadily, with their legs widely spread to compensate for poor balance. They may be uncoordinated and have trouble reaching for objects or making precise movements with their hands.

Mixed CP is the name given to cases that have symptoms from more than one of the types above.

Levels of Impairment

Another way to think about the varieties of CP is to look at what impairments a person faces in daily life. The Gross Motor Function Classification System recognizes five levels of impairment. Level 1 is the least impaired—it refers to kids who can walk and climb stairs well, though they may be slow or uncoordinated when running or jumping. Level 2 kids may not be able to run or jump, but they can walk without difficulty except on uneven surfaces or slopes. They can climb stairs as long as they can hold onto a railing.

At the third level, kids can walk using an assistive device, but they may need a wheelchair to go long distances or walk on tricky surfaces. They may be able to use their arms to propel the wheelchair. Level 4 kids generally require a wheelchair to get around. The wheelchair must either be motorized or pushed by somebody else. At level 5, the most severe degree of impairment, kids cannot move around independently at all, so they must be transported from place to place.

About one-third of kids with CP have trouble walking or are unable to walk. Another 11–12 percent can walk using supports, like handheld crutches or a wheeled walker. More than half of kids with cerebral palsy can walk independently.

Treatments

There is no known way of healing the brain injuries that cause CP. It is a chronic illness, which means that it lasts a person's whole life. But there are many ways to treat the symptoms and impairments of CP, including the following:

- **Physical therapy.** Regular exercises strengthen muscles, allowing a kid to make the most of his or her abilities. Physical therapy also creates better coordination, balance, and muscle tone. Kids learn to use mobility aids, like crutches and wheelchairs, or orthotic devices, which are braces or splints that keep muscles stretched out and better positioned.
- **Occupational therapy.** Focused on upper-body skills, this kind of therapy helps a kid find ways to perform everyday tasks, like getting dressed and moving around safely.
- **Speech and language therapy.** This type of therapy develops the muscles of the mouth, tongue, and throat so that kids can chew and swallow

A boy with CP gets some help on the monkey bars.

food, or speak more clearly. If impairments prevent kids from speaking, speech therapists teach them how to use communication aids. A young child or a person with an intellectual disability might point at pictures or icons on a board to express simple needs and thoughts. Other people with CP might us a computerized voice synthesizer to speak.

- **Medications.** Several different drugs treat muscles that are stiff, tight, contracted, or hyperactive. One type of muscle relaxant, baclofen, is

CO-OCCURRING CONDITIONS

These conditions and disorders are more commonly found in kids with CP than in people who don't have CP:

- Vision problems, including blurry vision, partial blindness, and strabismus (eyes that cross instead of looking straight ahead).
- Hearing loss.
- Speech and language disorders. Many kids with CP have trouble speaking. But a speech disorder doesn't mean a kid is intellectually disabled. Speech disorders are not related to intelligence.
- Involuntary drooling.
- Learning disabilities.
- Problems with depth perception and spatial awareness.
- Intellectual disabilities affect 30–50 percent of people with CP.
- Incontinence (weak bladder control).
- Epilepsy (seizures).
- Scoliosis and other abnormalities of the spine.
- Being unusually small or short for their age.
- Delayed puberty.

available via a surgically implanted pump that injects it directly into the fluid around the spine, making the muscles of the legs and torso less spastic. Another type of drug, commonly called botox, is injected into affected muscles once every few months. People with CP may also take medications to relieve pain, control seizures, or strengthen weak bones.

- **Surgery.** To treat overactive muscles, chronic pain, or problems with bladder control, surgeons may perform a selective dorsal rhizotomy. This involves cutting most of the nerves that send messages to affected muscles. Afterward, the muscles can respond more effectively to a person's will to move. **Orthopedic** surgery fixes problems with a kid's posture or gait. The impairments caused by CP can force a person's hips to shift around abnormally, making it even more difficult to walk. Surgery can correct the placement of the hips. Surgery is also used to correct spinal deformities like scoliosis.

Text-Dependent Questions

1. What are risk factors? What are some risk factors for CP?
2. If most cases of CP are congenital, why are they often not diagnosed until a baby is older?
3. What is the most common type of CP? Which is the most disabling type?

Research Project

A 2016 fashion show featured clothing designed especially for the needs of people with disabilities. You can watch a video about the fashion show here: www.youtube.com/watch?v=u4J7SXZQPj4. Can you think of a way to redesign a piece of clothing, a tool, or a piece of furniture to make it more useful for someone with CP? Draw or describe your design.

WORDS TO UNDERSTAND

amnesia: though it's popularly understood to mean forgetting your own identity, amnesia means a loss of memory of any kind.

cognitive function: the ability to think and process information.

coma: a state of deep unconsciousness.

postmortem: a medical examination of a dead body to determine the cause of death.

CHAPTER THREE

Traumatic Brain Injury

Maybe you collided with another player during a soccer game, and your head hit the turf hard. Maybe the car in front of you stopped suddenly, and your head snapped forward when the person driving you slammed on the brakes. Maybe you were horsing around with some friends on a second-floor balcony, and you accidentally fell to the ground.

All of these scenarios can result in a traumatic brain injury. TBIs can be caused by accidents or violence, like assaults, gunshot injuries, and explosions. But it's not always so dramatic—a TBI can be a concussion caused by a bump to the head. That may keep you out of school and away from strenuous activity for a little while. But, with proper care, treatment, and rest, a single concussion generally won't have a lasting effect on the rest of a person's life.

The same can't be said of more severe TBIs. These can wreak havoc on a person's life, causing long-term or permanent changes in a person's behavior, emotional stability, and even personality. They can leave a person with chronic headaches, memory lapses, or difficulty making sense of information.

Yadier Molina, a catcher for the St. Louis Cardinals, suffered a concussion in 2008.

A severe TBI can remove a person's ability to see, hear, or move around independently. A severe TBI can cause long-lasting loss of consciousness. In the very worst cases, it can kill.

Every year, more than 6,000 kids and teenagers die as a result of TBIs, making them the leading cause of death in this age group. These tragedies bring heartache for families, friends, and communities around the country. But for every TBI-related death, there are thousands of injuries resulting in temporary or permanent disability. Nearly half a million kids receive emergency medical care for TBIs every year. Each one of those kids may face days, weeks, months, or even years of coping with the effects of TBI. That's why it's so important to learn as much as we can about these injuries.

TBI, from Mild to Severe

You will hear concussions described as a mild form of TBI. But don't be fooled: when it comes to brain injuries, "mild" doesn't mean "not a big deal."

Falls are the leading cause of brain injury.

THE GLASGOW COMA SCALE

Developed in Scotland in 1974, the Glasgow Coma Scale is used by health-care professionals to quickly evaluate the severity of an injury to the brain. It looks at a person's ability to respond across three categories: eyes, speech, and movement. People who can open their eyes when spoken to, answer questions, or move around normally get a higher score than those who can't do these things.

A score of 13–15 on this scale is a mild TBI. A moderate TBI receives a score between 9–12. Any score of 8 or lower is a severe TBI resulting in a **coma**, a state of unconsciousness.

The categories of mild TBI, moderate TBI, and severe TBI don't describe how serious the injury might turn out to be. Instead, they refer to the time immediately following the injury, when a person loses consciousness or experiences a disruption in **cognitive function**, as measured by certain evaluative tests, like the Glasgow Coma Scale.

A mild TBI causes a person to lose consciousness for less than 30 minutes. Moderate TBI results in unconsciousness lasting from 30 minutes up to 6 hours. In severe TBI, a person remains unconscious for longer than 6 hours. The symptoms of cognitive dysfunction can last longer still. No matter how long symptoms last, however, you should always take them seriously.

What do these symptoms look like? You probably know what a loss of consciousness is. Someone who has fallen to the ground and doesn't respond or seem aware of anything going has lost consciousness. But what does a disruption in cognitive function look like? There's no single answer, but what it means is that a person's brain doesn't work as well as it normally should.

People experiencing cognitive dysfunction generally can't focus, understand, or remember things the way they normally do.

It's easy to tell when someone loses consciousness. But changes in cognitive function may be less obvious. A football player who receives a hard hit during practice might stay conscious. But that doesn't guarantee that he's fine. He may still have a concussion. For example, if he can't remember the hit, or the events immediately before the hit, he is experiencing a type of cognitive dysfunction called **amnesia**. If he seems confused about his teammates' names, or about which direction he should be running, these are also signs that he may be suffering from a concussion.

Concussions

Concussion are the most commonly reported kind of TBI. In a concussion, the force or blow causes immediate damage to brain cells at a scale too small to be visible on a brain scan. But this small-scale damage can add up to big problems. Injuries to individual brain cells create chemical changes inside the brain that affect its ability to function. These injuries make the brain more vulnerable to further injury later down the line. That's why someone with a concussion has to take extra time to rest and allow the brain to fully recover.

Remember, after a concussion, the physical structures of the brain may not look any different. What changes is how your brain works. These changes may appear immediately

EDUCATIONAL VIDEO

Scan this code to watch a video about TBI.

upon receiving the concussion. But they may also appear minutes, hours, or even up to a few days later. If you or someone you care about receives a concussion, it's important to pay attention to any changes you observe in focus, attention, emotional state, or behavior for several days afterward. Here are some things to watch for if you receive a concussion:

- A headache, or an uncomfortable feeling like something is pressing on your head.
- Seeing double, or having blurry vision.
- Feeling nauseous, or like you need to throw up.
- Dizziness.
- Difficulty walking in a straight line or keeping your balance.
- Sounds seem too loud or lights seem too bright.
- You can't concentrate or pay attention.
- Things don't seem to make sense.
- You have trouble remembering things.
- You feel weird, like you're wandering around in a fog.
- You're tired or fatigued.
- You can't put your finger on it exactly, but you just don't feel right.

If someone you know receives a concussion, watch for these possible changes in how he or she acts:

- They seem dazed, or out of it.
- They can't remember things that just happened, especially right around the hit or blow to the head.
- They have trouble following directions from coaches, teachers, or others.
- They seem unusually clumsy.
- They get intensely emotional in ways that you don't usually see them do. Sudden bursts of anger, irritation, anxiety, or sadness are common.

Even "minor" concussions should be checked out by a doctor, because small amounts of damage can accumulate over time.

Someone with a concussion should be seen by a health-care professional right away, even if there's no loss of consciousness. Your doctor will give you instructions about how to give your brain the best chance to heal following a concussion. Generally, you should expect to take it easy until your symptoms get better. That might mean staying home from school for a couple of days, and getting plenty of rest. You might be advised to avoid reading, looking at a TV or video screen, or trying to do any work that involves concentrating or thinking hard. Your doctor may also want you to skip sports practices, competitions, and other physical activities for a while, especially any activities that might cause you to receive another concussion.

It's really important that you follow your doctor's instructions. If you injure your brain a second time while still recovering from the effects of a previous concussion, you are at much higher risk for developing a severe brain injury. Even after you have fully recovered, you have a higher risk of serious injury to your brain if you sustain another concussion. In fact, the risk rises with every subsequent concussion. Recent research has found that repeated concussions and related inflammation can add up to severe damage to the brain, damage that gets progressively worse over time. Athletes who suffer a series of concussions over the course of their careers may develop a very serious degenerative brain disease called chronic traumatic encephalopathy (CTE).

Serious Traumatic Brain Injuries

A head wound that leaves visible damage is an obvious sign of a potentially severe TBI. Everyone knows to call 911 if a motor vehicle crash or violent assault leaves a victim with a penetrating TBI. But not all serious brain injuries are so easy to see. Like the injuries that can cause CTE, some types of serious brain damage result from non-penetrating TBI—injuries that may only be apparent on a brain scan. These injuries may happen right away, or they may develop hours or days after the original injury occurred. These are some of the symptoms to look for in persons who have suffered a bad fall, blow, or crash:

- The pupils in the eyes are different sizes, or don't match.
- There is a loss of consciousness, even if it's only for a minute or two. But longer periods of unconsciousness indicate worse injuries.
- They can't seem to stay awake, or can't be awakened.

ATHLETES AND CTE

The condition called CTE (chronic traumatic encephalopathy) was first recognized in boxers who had taken multiple blows to the head. But in 2005, a doctor named Bennet Omalu examined some tissue taken after death from the brain of a former NFL player named Mike Webster. Before his death, Webster had behaved erratically, showing signs of amnesia and dementia. Omalu found brain damage consistent with CTE in Webster's brain.

Since then, many current and former football players have revealed that they suffer from the symptoms of CTE. **Postmortems** of the brains of some players from the NFL, college, and even high school levels have confirmed that they had CTE. This discovery has led to calls for sports teams to figure out more effective ways to prevent concussions and other TBIs.

BRAIN REST

Doctors and scientists still don't know very much about how the brain changes that result from a concussion. There are no pills or medications you can take to make your brain recover more quickly or easily. For now, doctors recommend that you rest as much as possible following a concussion. Your doctor may also suggest an over-the-counter pain reliever if you're suffering from headaches.

It might be hard to have to sit out from school, sports, or other things you enjoy while you're recovering from a concussion. Take care of yourself after a brain injury, even when it's boring. Remember, a little boredom now can give you the chance to enjoy activities and excitement for the rest of your life.

- When they talk, their speech is garbled or slurred.
- They describe feelings of numbness or weakness in their arms or legs.
- They are suddenly very uncoordinated.
- They vomit or feel nauseous.
- They have a bad headache that gets worse rather than going away.
- They display uncontrollable movements, like convulsions or seizures.
- They seem uncharacteristically upset, restless, or agitated, like they're having trouble sitting still.
- They are confused, or behaving oddly.

Any one of the above symptoms is a reason to get emergency medical care right away. They may be signs that the person has developed a hematoma or hemorrhage. They may also be a sign that the original injury has led to swelling or fluid pressing on the brain, and possibly cutting off the brain's oxygen supply. Quick medical care is key. It gives a person with a serious TBI the best possible chance at recovery.

Text-Dependent Questions

1. What are the differences between mild, moderate, and severe TBI?
2. List five symptoms of a concussion.
3. What's the best way to take care of yourself if you have a concussion?

Research Project

Find out what your school's sports program does to reduce the likelihood of TBIs. Have any rules been changed in recent years, in response to our improved understanding of TBIs? Write a brief report about what your school is doing to keep student athletes safer.

WORDS TO UNDERSTAND

microcephaly: an abnormally small head due to a halt in or reduction of brain development.

neurological: relating to the nervous system (including the brain and spinal cord).

CHAPTER FOUR

Living with CP or TBI

A mild brain injury can turn your life upside-down for a couple of weeks, but permanent damage to the brain affects the rest of your life. A brain injury might prevent you from getting around independently. It may restrict your ability to use your arms and hands. Brain injuries can rob you of your memory and sap your ability to learn. They can make it hard for you to speak and communicate. They can make you sad, angry, impulsive, depressed, or anxious. In short, brain injuries can alter almost anything about your life.

Kids who suffer a brain injury at or before birth face any or all of these obstacles every day for their entire lives. Other kids and teenagers who receive a serious TBI cross a stark dividing line between their lives before their injuries and their lives afterward. Many people with congenital brain injuries or brain injuries acquired later in life go on to overcome these challenges and accomplish wonderful things. What kids with **neurological** injuries need are the same things we all need: respectful, encouraging, accessible environments that give us the chance to reach our highest potential.

Kids with CP may need a little extra help with physical challenges such as climbing stairs or getting on and off buses.

Accessibility and Bullying

Every kid with a brain injury has his or her own set of individual needs and strengths. But some issues are widely shared by many people with conditions like cerebral palsy and TBI. Accessibility is one of the most important issues. Think about your school. How many flights of stairs does it have? Are there other ways to get from one place to another besides using the stairs? How much longer does it take to use one of those alternate routes, and can it be done in the time you're given to get from one place to the next? All of these are potential obstacles that someone who uses a walker, crutches, or a wheelchair has to think about every day.

Now think about your community and the places that you go most regularly. Someone with mobility issues has to consider how far a walk it is from the parking area or the nearest public transportation stop to the entrance of the place. Are there sidewalks or paved paths? Is there a curb cut, or gentle slope to make it easier for someone in a wheelchair to get on and off the sidewalk? Are there stairs at the entrance? Are there stairs inside? Are hallways or passageways wide enough to accommodate a wheelchair? The answers to any of these questions can make places difficult or even impossible to reach for a person with mobility issues.

People with limited use of their arms and hands may have other needs. For example, a kid who isn't able to manage writing with a pen or pencil might use a specially equipped computer to take notes or write papers. Technology can assist kids in doing many things, but people with limited use of their arms and hands still have to come up with solutions for dilemmas they face every day. Try buttoning your jeans, squeezing toothpaste onto your toothbrush, or opening a milk carton in the school cafeteria with only one hand. It takes creativity and determination to work around these kinds of limitations, but people with cerebral palsy and other brain injuries that affect movement do it every day. The same is true for kids and teens with other disabilities related to brain injuries. People who have difficulties speaking, seeing, or hearing also have to find new and creative ways to participate in activities that other kids might take for granted.

Could your school be doing more to make activities more accessible?

Teasing, bullying, or being deliberately excluded are problems faced by many kids and teens with cerebral palsy or other brain injuries. The good news is that you can help solve these problems. You can always choose to be the person who is kind, helpful, and inclusive — and you can stand up to bullies who are cruel to anyone for being different or having a disability.

When a Family Member Has a TBI

Someone who has suffered a TBI may seem almost like a different person sometimes. These individuals might forget about things you were supposed to do together. They might get irritated easily. They might seem depressed. Maybe they stay in bed sometimes when everyone else is doing things. They might have trouble going to work, or be unable to work. They might get mad if you make a lot of noise or turn on the lights. Maybe they often tell you to leave them alone.

If you have a parent or a sibling who is living with the effects of a TBI, you may feel sad or scared about how the person you love has changed. You might worry if things will ever go back to the way they used to be. These feelings are totally normal. It might help to talk about your feelings with someone you trust, like another adult in your family, or a counselor at school. A doctor may be able to help you find other people in your community who understand what you're going through.

MILITARY VETERANS AND TBIs

Between 14 and 20 percent of all combat injuries incurred by members of the armed services involve a TBI. Most of these brain injuries are concussions, but they may result in more serious or long-lasting injuries. This is particularly true of TBIs caused by exposure to shockwaves from an explosion. Shockwaves don't necessarily leave any visible sign of damage. Soldiers focused on succeeding at their missions might not notice the symptoms of a TBI until later.

For kids whose parents or other family members return from a military deployment with a TBI, there can be big changes at home. Many military bases and health facilities offer support programs for veterans with TBIs and their families. If you need some help coping with changes at home, these programs might be able to point you in the right direction.

Preventing Brain Injuries

You know that brain injuries can change, devastate, or even end a person's life. But did you know that many brain injuries are preventable? You can take steps to reduce the risk of brain injuries. Here are some simple things you can do:

- Always wear a seat belt with a shoulder harness when you're riding in a car or other vehicle. If there's a crash, these safety restraints can keep your head protected from the worst shocks.

- Wear a helmet when you ride a skateboard, scooter, bicycle, or all-terrain vehicle. If you fall at high speeds, a helmet will protect your head from the force of the impact, and it will shield you from a skull fracture or penetrating TBI.

- If you play football, lacrosse, or hockey, always wear your safety gear. Never try to play through a blow to the head. A concussion can make you clumsy and confused, increasing the risk that you'll receive another concussion just

Sometimes people avoid helmets while playing sports because they don't look cool, but the potential for long-term damage makes helmets very important.

when your brain is least able to handle the damage. Studies show that players who take more hits to the head are more likely to suffer from degenerative brain disease later in life—and the damaging effects can show up as early as high school. Take your future seriously. Always protect your head!

EDUCATIONAL VIDEO

Scan this code to watch a video about two athletes talking about life after TBI.

- The same advice holds true no matter what sport you play. Cheerleading, basketball, and soccer are three leading causes of concussions among youth athletes. Any sport that allows physical contact between players can result in a TBI. Protect your head, and support your teammates in protecting theirs.

- Do you babysit, or have younger brothers or sisters? Falls are one of the most common causes of head injury in very young children. Make sure little kids stay safe around potential hazards such as open windows, stairs, and playground equipment.

- Falls are also a major risk for elderly people. Don't leave things lying around on the floor where an elderly person might trip on them.

- Never play around with a gun or firearm. Gunshot wounds cause deadly head injuries.

- Don't play into the cycle of violence, especially as you enter the years between the ages of 15 and 24, when violent assaults are a major cause of TBI, particularly in boys and men.

- Get vaccinated. When you protect yourself from diseases like German measles (rubella), you also help make sure those diseases won't spread to pregnant women. That stops one known cause of cerebral palsy in its tracks.

EMERGING THREATS TO BRAINS

In 2015 the country of Brazil reported an unusually high number of newborn babies with **microcephaly,** or very small heads. Microcephaly occurs when the brain stops growing. It can be caused by some of the same infections that are related to CP, but none of those infections were circulating in higher numbers than usual in Brazil. So what was causing the epidemic of microcephaly?

The answer turns out to be the Zika virus. First discovered in 1947, it was considered rare and mild until clusters of cases linked it to birth defects like microcephaly. Spread by mosquitoes and by unprotected sex with an infected person, the Zika virus can now be found in a large number of countries, including the United States. Unless scientists can figure out how to halt Zika, we may witness a new generation of babies whose lives are forever altered by congenital brain damage.

Text-Dependent Questions

1. List three obstacles that someone with mobility issues might face.
2. What should you always do when riding in a motor vehicle?
3. Why should you wear a helmet when you're riding a bike?

Research Project

Read "Shelby's Story," about a high school cheerleader who suffered two concussions in the space of a few months. It is available on the CDC website, at www.cdc.gov/headsup/pdfs/stories/shelby_story-a.pdf. What changes occurred to her as a result of her TBI? What changes were made in her sport? Write a brief report addressing these issues.

FURTHER READING

Centers for Disease Control and Prevention. "HEADS UP." https://www.cdc.gov/HeadsUp/.

Cerebral Palsy Foundation. "Fact Sheet Library." http://yourcpf.org/what-is-cp/.

Draper, Sharon M. *Out of My Mind.* New York: Atheneum Books for Young Readers, 2010.

Goldsmith, Connie. *Traumatic Brain Injury: From Concussion to Coma.* Minneapolis: Twenty-First Century Books, 2014.

McCormick, Patricia. *Purple Heart.* New York: Balzer & Bray, 2016.

Philip, Aaron, with Tonya Bolden. *This Kid Can Fly: It's about Ability (Not Disability).* New York: Balzer & Bray, 2016.

Rao, Vani, and Sandeep Vaishnavi. *The Traumatized Brain: A Family Guide to Understanding Mood, Memory, and Behavior After Brain Injury.* A Johns Hopkins Press Health Book. Baltimore, MD: Johns Hopkins University Press, 2015.

Shusterman, Michele P. *The Cerebral Palsy Tool Kit: From Diagnosis to Understanding.* Greenville, SC: CP NOW, 2015.

Educational Videos

Chapter One: CrashCourse. "Central Nervous System." https://youtu.be/q8NtmDrb_qo?list=PL8dPuuaLjXtOAKed_MxxWBNaPno5h3Zs8.

Chapter Two: KidsHealth. "Living with CP: Ira's Story." https://youtu.be/T3un46eTNbo.

Chapter Three: NICHD Videos. "Traumatic Brain Injury in Kids." https://youtu.be/OiLBPsTRLnQ.

Chapter Four: CDC Foundation TBI. "Get a Heads Up: Severe Brain Injury." https://youtu.be/moWCAUSuXzo.

SERIES GLOSSARY

accommodation: an arrangement or adjustment to a new situation; for example, schools make accommodations to help students cope with illness.

anemia: an illness caused by a lack of red blood cells.

autoimmune: type of disorder where the body's immune system attacks the body's tissues instead of germs.

benign: not harmful.

biofeedback: a technique used to teach someone how to control some bodily functions.

capillaries: tiny blood vessels that carry blood from larger blood vessels to body tissues.

carcinogens: substances that can cause cancer to develop.

cerebellum: the back part of the brain; it controls movement.

cerebrum: the front part of the brain; it controls many higher-level thinking and functions.

cholesterol: a waxy substance associated with fats that coats the inside of blood vessels, causing cardiovascular disease.

cognitive: related to conscious mental activities, such as learning and thinking.

communicable: transferable from one person to another.

congenital: a condition or disorder that exists from birth.

correlation: a connection between different things that suggests they may have something to do with one another.

dominant: in genetics, a dominant trait is expressed in a child even when the trait is only inherited from one parent.

environmental factors: anything that affects how people live, develop, or grow. Climate, diet, and pollution are examples.

genes: units of hereditary information.

hemorrhage: bleeding from a broken blood vessel.

hormones: substances the body produces to instruct cells and tissues to perform certain actions.

inflammation: redness, swelling, and tenderness in a part of the body in response to infection or injury.

insulin: a hormone produced in the pancreas that controls cells' ability to absorb glucose.

lymphatic system: part of the human immune system; transports white blood cells around the body.

malignant: harmful; relating to tumors, likely to spread.

mutation: a change in the structure of a gene; some mutations are harmless, but others may cause disease.

neurological: relating to the nervous system (including the brain and spinal cord).

neurons: specialized cells found in the central nervous system (the brain and spinal cord).

occupational therapy: a type of therapy that teaches one how to accomplish tasks and activities in daily life.

oncology: the study of cancer.

orthopedic: dealing with deformities in bones or muscles.

prevalence: how common or uncommon a disease is in any given population.

prognosis: the forecast for the course of a disease that predicts whether a person with the disease will get sicker, recover, or stay the same.

progressive disease: a disease that generally gets worse as time goes on.

psychomotor: relating to movement or muscle activity resulting from mental activity.

recessive: in genetics, a recessive trait will only be expressed if a child inherits it from both parents.

remission: an improvement in or disappearance of someone's symptoms of disease; unlike a cure, remission is usually temporary.

resilience: the ability to bounce back from difficult situations.

seizure: an event caused by unusual brain activity resulting in physical or behavior changes.

syndrome: a condition with a set of associated symptoms.

ulcers: a break or sore in skin or tissue where cells disintegrate and die. Infections may occur at the site of an ulcer.

INDEX

Illlustrations are indicated by page numbers in *italic* type.

A

abuse, 27

accessibility, 49, *50*, 51, *52*

accidents, *17*, 27, 37

acquired cerebral palsy, 27

amnesia, 36, 41, 45

anger, 27, 42, 49

anxiety, 14, 42, 49

arachnoid mater, 13, 19

assistive technology, *29*, 30, 32

ataxia, 22, 23

ataxic CP, 31

athetoid, 22, 31

athletes, *14*, 44–45, 55

atrophy, 20

axons, 8, 9, 19

B

babies, 15, 20, 23, 25, 26, 27–28, 56

baclofen, 34, 35

balance, 31, 32, 42

behavior, 14, 37, 42

birth defects, 25, 56

bladder control, 34, 35

bleeding, 13, 16, 19

blows, 16–17, 19, 27, 41, 42, 44–45, 54

botox, 34, 35

brain, the, 8–21

   background, 9

   damage of Richard III, 20

   injuries, 13–19, 21

   inside the, 10–13

brain injury, living with, 48–56

   accessibility and bullying, 51–52

   background, 49

   family members, 52

   preventing, 54–55

   veterans, 53

   Zika virus and, 56

brain rest, 41, 43, 46

Brazil, 56

bruises (contusions), 8, 19

bullying, 52

C

capillaries, 8, 19

car accidents, *17*

causes

   of brain injuries, 14

   of cerebral palsy, 25–26

   of concussions, 55

cell replacement, 13

cerebral cortex, 12, 15, 25

cerebral palsy (CP), 15, 20, 22–35

   acquired, 27

   background, 23

   causes, 25–26

   diagnosis and symptoms, 26, 27–28, 29

   impairments, 31–32

   risk factors, 23, 25

   treatments, 32, 34, 35

   types of, 29–30, 31

cerebrum, 12

choreic, 22, 31

chronic headaches, 37

chronic traumatic encephalopathy (CTE), 44, 45

cognitive function, 36, 40–41

coma, 36, 40

combat injuries, 53

communication, 9, 31, 34, 49

community, 51

computed tomography (CT), 28

concussions, 15, 17, 37, 39, 40–44, 55

congenital brain damage, 8, 15, 16–17, 27, 56

consciousness, 38, 40, 43

contracture, 22, 26

contrecoup lesions, 19

contusions (bruises), 8, 19

co–occurring conditions, 34, 35

Cooper, Prya, 24

coping, 39, 53

coup lesions, 19

cranial ultrasound, 28

curb cuts, 51

cytomegalovirus, 26

D

damage, brain, 13–17, 19–20, 25–27, 31, 41, 44, 49

deaths from TBIs, 15, 38

degenerative brain disease, 44, 55

dementia, 45

dendrites, 8, 9

depression, 14, 49, 52

depth perception, 31

diagnosis, 28, 34, 42, 44, 46

diffuse axonal injuries (DAIs), 19

diffuse injuries, 8, 17

disabilities, 15

drooling, 31, 34

dura mater, 13, 19

dyskinetic CP, 31

E

edema, 21

effects of brain injuries, 13–14

elderly people, 55

emergency medical care, 46

emotions, 37, 42, 49

epidemic, 56

epidermal hematomas, 19

epilepsy, 31, 34

exclusion, 52

exercise, 32, 33

external forces, 16

F

falls, 39, 55

family members, 52–53

feelings, 14, 53

fetus, 15, 16, 25–26

fevers, 25

focal injury, 17

focus, 41, 42

G

gene mutations, 15–16, 26

German measles, 25, 55

Glasgow Coma Scale, 40

glial cells, 8, 12, 26

gray matter, 12

Gross Motor Function Classification System, 31–32

gunshot wounds, 55

H

headaches, 42, 46

hearing, 31, 34, 38, 51

helmets, 54

hematomas, 8, 19, 21, 46

hemiparesis, spastic, 30

hemiplegia, spastic, 30

hemorrhages, 8, 19, 46

hypoxia, 22, 26

I

imaging, 27, 28
impairments, 13, 23, 31–32, 34, 35
independence, 32, 38, 49
infections, 16, 25–26, 56
injuries, 13–19, 21, 38–39
intelligence, 30, 31, 34
intracerebral hematoma, 19
ischemic injury, 22, 26

K

kids
    brain injuries in, 14–15
    with cerebral palsy, 25

L

language therapy, 32, 34
learning ability, 28, 32, 34, 49
Little, William John, 20

M

magnetic resonance imaging (MRI), 28
medications, 34, 35, 46
memory, 37, 49
meninges, 8, 13
microcephaly, 48, 56
mixed CP, 31
mobility, 32, 51
Molina, Yadier, 38
monitoring, 21
motor disabilities, 8, 15
muscles, 15, 23, 26, 29–31, 32

N

nerves, 8, 9
nervous system, 11
neurological injuries, 48, 49

neurons, 8, 9, 10–11, 12, 13, 19
neurotransmitters, 9, 19
non-penetrating TBIs, 16, 17, 19, 44–45
nutrients, 16, 26

O

obstacles, 51
occipital lobes, 13
occupational therapy, 32
oligodendrocytes, 26
Omalu, Bennet, 45
orthopedic surgery, 22, 35
orthotic devices, 22, 32
oxygen, 16, 26, 46

P

paralysis, 30
parasites, 26
paresis, 22, 30
penetrating TBIs, 16, 17
periventricular leukomalacia (PVL), 26
personality, 37
physical actions, 9
physical therapy, 32
pia mater, 13, 19
placenta, 26
-plegia, 22, 30
postmortems, 36, 45
pregnancy, 16, 25, 55
premature births, 25
prevention, 54–55
primary injury, 19, 21
puberty, 34

Q

quadriparesis, spastic, 30, 31
quadriplegia, spastic, 30, 31

R

recovery time, 19
Richard III, 20
risk factors, 23, 25
rotational forces, 19
rubella, 25, 55

S

sadness, 42, 49, 53
safety gear, 54
scans, brain, 27, 28, 41, 44
scoliosis, 20, 30, 34, 35
seat belts, 54
secondary injuries, 21
seeing, 13, 38, 42, 51
selective dorsal rhizotomy, 35
serious traumatic brain injuries,
    44–45
shaken baby syndrome, 27
Shakespeare
    Richard III, 20
shock waves, 19, 53
skull, 13, 16, 19
soldiers, 53
sound waves, 28
spasms, *30*
spastic CP, 29–31
special equipment, 51
speech, 30–31, 32, 34, 40, 46, 49, 51
sports injuries, *14,* 16, 17, *18,* 19, *54*
stability, 37
strokes, 22, 26
subarachnoid hemorrhages, 19
support programs, 53
surgery, 35
symptoms, 26, 27, 40–41, 44, 46

T

teasing, 52
technology, *29,* 51
thoughts, 9, 34
toxoplasmosis, 26
traumatic brain injuries (TBIs), 15, 16,
    36–47
    athletes and, 45
    background, 37, 38–39
    brain rest for, 46
    concussions, *38,* 41–44
    Glasgow Coma Scale, 40
    severity of, 39, 40–41, 44, 46–47
treatments, 32, 33, 35, 43–44

U

unconsciousness, 40, 44

V

vaccinations, 25, 55
veterans, 53
violence, 37, 55
vision problems, 34, 42
voluntary muscle movements, 9

W

walking, 31–32, 35
Webster, Mike, 45
wheelchairs, *24, 29,* 32, 51
white matter, 12

X

X-rays, 28

Z

Zika virus, 56

ABOUT THE ADVISOR

Heather Pelletier, Ph.D., is a pediatric staff psychologist at Rhode Island Hospital/Hasbro Children's Hospital with a joint appointment as a clinical assistant professor in the departments of Psychiatry and Human Behavior and Pediatrics at the Warren Alpert Medical School of Brown University. She is also the director of behavioral pain medicine in the division of Children's Integrative therapies, Pain management and Supportive care (CHIPS) in the department of Pediatrics at Hasbro Children's Hospital. Dr. Pelletier provides clinical services to children in various medical specialty clinics at Hasbro Children's Hospital, including the pediatric gastroenterology, nutrition, and liver disease clinics.

ABOUT THE AUTHOR

Rebecca Sherman writes about health care policy, public health issues, and parenting. She lives in Massachusetts with her family.

PHOTO CREDITS

28 DAY BOOK
Hewlett-Woodmere Public Library
Hewlett, New York 11557-0903

Business Phone 516-374-1967
Recorded Announcements 516-374-1667
Website www.hwpl.org